Tubas

Music Makers

T H E   C H I L D ' S   W O R L D ®,   I N C .

Tubas

Bob Temple

THE CHILD'S WORLD®, INC.

On the cover: This man buzzes his lips as he plays his tuba.

Published in the United States of America by The Child's World®, Inc.
PO Box 326
Chanhassen, MN 55317-0326
800-599-READ
www.childsworld.com

Product Manager Mary Berendes
Editor Katherine Stevenson, Ph.D.

Library of Congress Cataloging-in-Publication Data
Temple, Bob.
Tubas / by Bob Temple.
     p. cm.
Includes index.
ISBN 1-56766-046-0 (lib. bdg. : alk. paper)
1. Tuba—Juvenile literature. [1. Tuba.]   I. Title.
ML970 .T46 2002
788.9'8—dc21

                                    2001005994

Photo Credits
© Bob Daemmrich/Picturequest: 6
© Bob Krist/CORBIS: 19
© Chip Henderson/IndexStock: 15, 16
© Christian Michaels/FPG International: 9
© Jim Bounds/AP: 10
© Kwame Zikomo/SuperStock: cover, 2
© PhotoDisc: 13
© PhotoDisc: 23 (except cornet photo)
© Richard Cummins/CORBIS: 20
© Siede Preis/Getty: 23 (cornet)

Table of Contents

As you sit and enjoy the orchestra's music, you hear a sound lower than all the others. Near the back of the group, you see musicians holding large, heavy-looking instruments. These are the instruments making the low sounds. What are these strange instruments? They're tubas!

← This man is playing a tuba at an outdoor concert.

Brass Instruments

There are many different types of instruments. **Wind instruments** make a sound when you air blow into them. **Brass instruments** are wind instruments made of metal. On most brass instruments, you can change the sound by pressing down on different buttons, or **valves**. Tubas are brass instruments. So are trumpets and French horns.

This man is playing his tuba with a street band. →

How Old Are Tubas?

Tubas were invented so that brass bands would have a low-sounding, or **bass**, instrument. The first tuba was produced in 1835. Soon, tubas were being made in a variety of shapes and sizes. Each of these tubas was given a different name. Sousaphones and baritones are two popular kinds of tuba.

← This man owns a tuba shop in North Carolina. Almost every kind of tuba can be found in his store.

Along the tube are the valves that change the sounds the tuba makes. At the far end, the tube opens into a wide **bell** where the air and the sound come out.

This woman presses on the tuba's valves as she plays. →

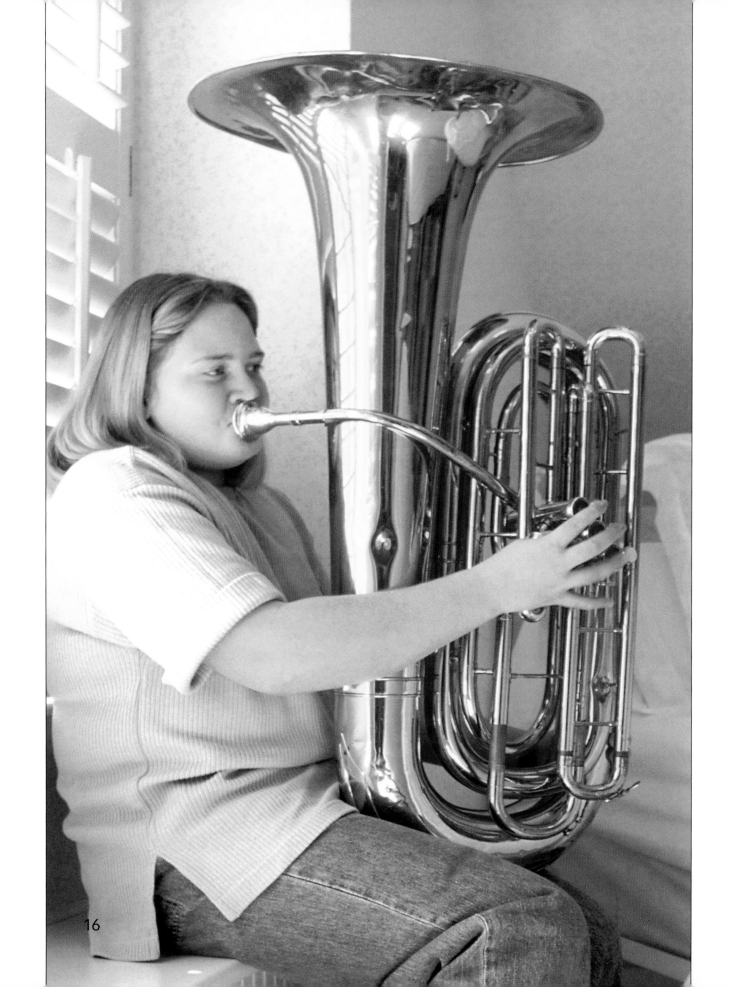

Tubas are huge instruments. If you straightened out its curved tube, a tuba would be 16 feet long! When you play a tuba, you must wrap your arms around the tuba to hold it.

← This girl is holding her tuba on her lap as she practices.   17

Sousaphones are the kind of tuba you usually see in marching bands. Their tubing forms a large circle that wraps around the player's shoulder and body. Resting the tubing on one shoulder makes the instrument easier to carry. On most tubas, the bell points upward, but on a sousaphone, it points to the front.

These men are playing sousaphones in Puerto Rico. →

How Do You Play a Tuba?

To play a tuba, you press your lips together tightly and hold them to the mouthpiece. Then you blow air into the mouthpiece, making your lips buzz, or **vibrate**. Pressing the valves makes the tuba play different sounds, or **notes**. Changing the shape of your lips changes the sound, too.

← You can see how this man uses his lips to push air through the tuba's mouthpiece.

How Are Tubas Used?

Tubas are an important part of many orchestras and bands. Most orchestras have tubas and baritones. Marching bands usually have sousaphones. But whenever you hear that low OOM-PAH OOM-PAH sound, you can be sure it's being made by some type of tuba!

Other Brass Instruments

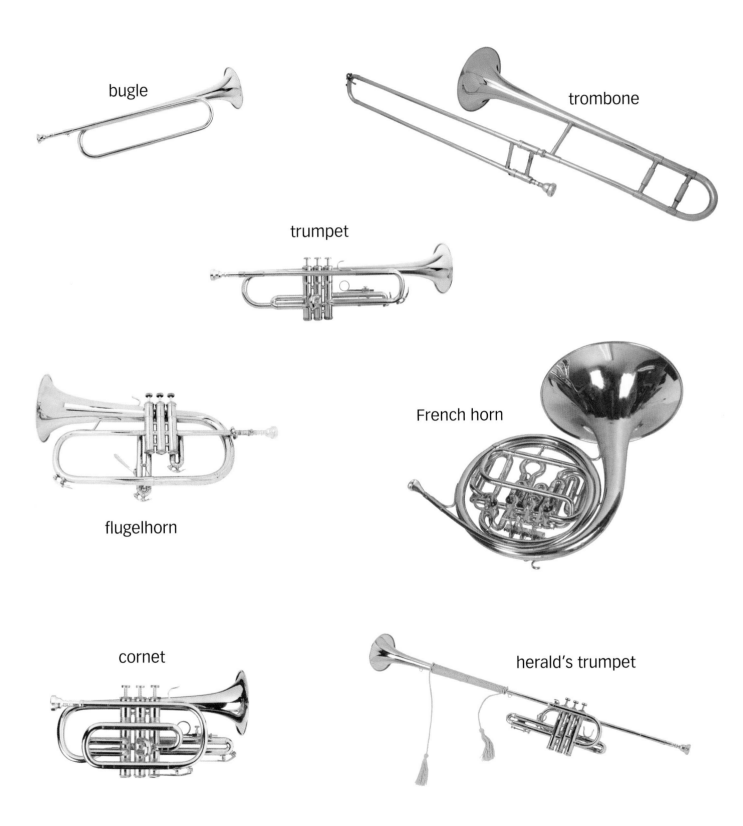

bugle

trombone

trumpet

French horn

flugelhorn

cornet

herald's trumpet

Glossary

bass (BASE)
Bass is a deep or low sound. Tubas were invented to add a bass sound to brass bands.

bell (BELL)
On a brass instrument, the bell is the wider end where the sound comes out. Tubas have a very large bell.

brass instruments (BRASS IN-struh-ments)
Brass instruments are metal instruments that you play by blowing air through them and pressing valves to change the sound. Tubas are brass instruments.

mouthpiece (MOWTH-peece)
On a brass instrument, the mouthpiece is the place where you put your mouth to play. Tubas have a large, cup-shaped mouthpiece.

notes (NOHTS)
Notes are musical sounds. On tubas, you produce different notes by pressing the valves.

valves (VALVZ)
On a brass instrument, valves are buttons you press to change the sound. Tubas have valves.

vibrate (VY-brate)
When something vibrates, it moves back and forth very quickly. To play a tuba, you vibrate your lips against the mouthpiece as you blow into it.

wind instruments (WIND IN-struh-ments)
Wind instruments are instruments that produce a sound when you blow air through them. Tubas are wind instruments.

Index